NEWCASTLE-UNDER-LYME IN 50 BUILDINGS

MERVYN EDWARDS

AMBERLEY

Acknowledgements

The author would like to thank Ron Chadwick, Kenneth Edwards, Jacques Fielding, Norman Scholes, Gary Tudor and the staff at Newcastle Library. Every effort has been made to correctly identify the copyright owners of the photographic materials used in this book. If, inadvertently, credits have not been correctly acknowledged, we apologise and promise to make the necessary corrections in reprinted editions.

First published 2019

Amberley Publishing, The Hill, Stroud
Gloucestershire GL5 4EP

www.amberley-books.com

British Library Cataloguing in Publication Data.
A catalogue record for this book is available from the British Library.

ISBN 978 1 4456 9183 1 (print)
ISBN 978 1 4456 9184 8 (ebook)

Typesetting by Aura Technology and Software Services, India.
Printed in Great Britain.

Contents

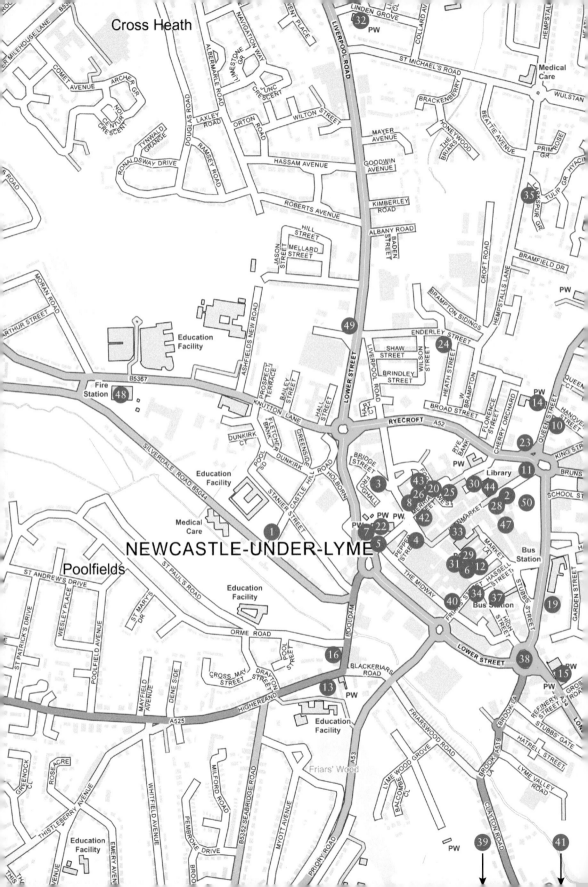

Key

1. Castle Wall (remnant), John O'Gaunt's Road
2. Former Golden Ball pub, Bridge Street
3. Former St Giles' Rectory, Ironmarket
4. Former Wine Vaults Public House, High Street
5. Brick façade of the Former Pomona Works
6. Guildhall, High Street
7. Unitarian Meeting House, off Church Street
8. Former Newcastle Conservative Club, Merrial Street
9. The Polite Vicar pub and restaurant, Etruria Road
10. Former Mic House, Queen Street
11. Former Lace Gentlemen's Club, Ironmarket
12. Former Castle Hotel frontage (in part), High Street
13. Higherland Methodist Church, Higherland
14. St George's Church, Queen Street
15. Holy Trinity Church, London Road
16. Former Orme School, Orme Road
17. Pitfield House, Brampton Park
18. The Firs, Brampton Park
19. Militia Barracks, Barracks Road
20. Former Ebenezer Chapel, Ryecroft
21. Congregational Chapel, King Street
22. St Giles' Church, Church Lane
23. Wall and archway, Ryecroft/Queen Street
24. Former Bear Hotel, West Brampton
25. Ten Green Bottles, Merrial Street
26. Former Ebenezer Sunday School, Merrial Street
27. St Paul's Church, Victoria Road
28. Arnold Machin pub, Ironmarket
29. Former John O'Gaunt's Castle Inn, Stanier Street
30. Former Police Station, Merrial Street
31. Lancaster Buildings, High Street
32. St Michael and All Angels Church, Linden Grove, Cross Heath
33. Former Paulden's Department Store, High Street
34. Former Woolworth store
35. The Hollies Council Estate, Hempstalls Lane
36. Former Shakespeare, George Street
37. Former Market Arcade, High Street
38. Grosvenor Roundabout, High Street
39. St James' Church, Clayton
40. Midway Shops, Midway
41. The Holiday Inn (previously the Post House Hotel)
42. York Place Shopping Centre, Red Lion Square
43. Former Civic Offices, Merrial Street

44. Former Newcastle Library
45. New Victoria Theatre, Etruria Road
46. Former National Westminster Bank Regional HQ, the Brampton
47. Castle Walk Outdoor Shopping Area, off Ironmarket
48. Newcastle Community Fire Station, Knutton Road
49. The Cotton Mill pub, Liverpool Road
50. Castle House, Barracks Road

Introduction

Newcastle-under-Lyme Borough Council has produced several town guides over the years for the education and edification of both local people and visitors to the 'Loyal and Ancient Borough'.

Newcastle has every right to be proud of its history as a road communications centre, base for long-distance carriers, postal centre of the district, coaching stop, market town, retail capital and entertainment magnet. Its trade links with the adjacent Potteries were numerous, while some of the brightest minds in the six towns – such as Thomas Whieldon, Josiah Wedgwood and Josiah Spode – were intimately connected with bustling Newcastle before and during the rapid growth of the Potteries.

Given this context, we can see how necessary it is for Newcastle to preserve the finest and most historically important examples of its built environment. However, the reader-friendly, bright-and-breezy town guides, eye-catching interpretative boards in the town and other council-produced literature do not tell us the whole story of the changes to Newcastle's townscape that have taken place over the last sixty years.

The town centre reconstruction that occurred in the 1960s was an attempt by local government of the day to reinvigorate Newcastle and embrace an exciting future that would take advantage of new national road links. Beautiful Georgian and Victorian buildings were demolished as muscle-flexing Newcastle strove to rebrand itself as a retail destination. Decisions made by the public and private sector combined to rid the town of buildings such as the Municipal Hall, the Globe Hotel, the Castle Hotel and the Covered Market. To use the modern parlance, these buildings were no longer fit for purpose in the 'Brave New World' that was being created. Was something bold and visionary happening in Newcastle, or was the council guilty of a bull-at-a-gate, insensitive mindset in driving a bulldozer not only through its attractive main streets but also its precious past?

The decisions made during this period – which saw the inception of Newcastle Civic Society – still rankle with many Newcastilians of advancing years who wish to preserve the best of what's left.

However, in an era when cost-cutting is king, the townscape has continued to radically change. Tall gateway buildings such as the No. 1 London Road apartment block, the Brunswick Street apartments and the Castle House council headquarters tower over the town, while period buildings such as Newcastle police station and the old Civic Offices in Merrial Street stand derelict. The St Giles and

St George's School building was bulldozed in order to make way for Castle House, much to the consternation of many who love Newcastle.

The new high-rise apartments have been described by Newcastle Civic Society as unsympathetic to the rest of the town and not in keeping with its overall appearance. Indeed, in 2007, the society labelled Brunswick Court a 'design error'.

This book features buildings that say something about Newcastle's development through history. The entries have not necessarily been chosen on merit and some of the inclusions and exclusions may seem perverse, for which no apology is given. However, in focusing on the architecture of the town, this project offers a different perspective on its history.

The 50 Buildings

1. Castle Wall (Remnant), John O'Gaunt's Road, Late Twelfth Century/Early
Thirteenth Century

This remnant of wall was part of the medieval entranceway into the castle that gave Newcastle-under-Lyme its name. In the late twelfth or thirteenth century, the original wooden castle was rebuilt in stone and was discovered during excavations in 1935.

John O'Gaunt had so many estates that he rarely visited Newcastle, though he nevertheless maintained the castle until his death in 1399. John O'Gaunt's Road was the causeway across the castle pool, and the remains of the castle motte can be found to the rear of Queen Elizabeth Gardens, in nearby Silverdale Road.

Information on the castle and these excavations are widely available. However, given that this book will discuss disparate attitudes towards building preservation in Newcastle, it is appropriate to mention prevailing views on this historic remnant's value at the time of the excavation in 1935.

Alderman T. O. Harper viewed that in the year when the town was celebrating the 700th anniversary of the granting of its Guild Merchant charter, there should be no grumbles about spending a few pounds on something so closely associated with the origins and name of the town. The remnant, he declared, was of 'inestimable historical value'. He added that the financial arguments were less important than the need to preserve the wall for posterity: 'If they had a little imagination they might realise the historical value of the castle.'

However, reports of the meetings of the Newcastle Town Council show that there was opposition to the excavations, which were seen by some as a waste of ratepayers' money.

Mr George Scott said that he had never heard any reason why these 'few old stones' should be preserved, and that the proposed fence around the remnant might spoil the view of the adjacent school. Alderman A. Moran agreed. 'As far as he could see, there was nothing at all of historical value … if you dug up some stones anywhere else and called them John O'Gaunt's Castle, nobody would know the difference.'

Today, the wall remnant is indeed fenced and its history explained through an interpretative panel. However, debates about the relative importance of Newcastle's preserved history continue.

Right and below: Remnant of the castle wall, 2019.

2. Former Golden Ball Pub, Bridge Street, *c.* 1600

Newcastle Civic Society, whose blue plaque adorns the frontage, gives the date of *c.* 1600 as the building's date of origin. In 1822–23 the Golden Ball was being kept by Edward Foden, victualler, though it seems to have been well established by then as a watering hole. Its designation changed over the years, as listed in various documents and newspapers. For instance, when the Golden Ball was to let in 1846, it was 'that old established public house', then in the occupation of William Bates. Incidentally, brewing utensils were included in the sale. In 1861, however, it appears in the reports of the Newcastle petty sessions as the Golden Ball beerhouse, then kept by George Skinner, who was fined for trading during illegal hours. In 1869, it was described as a valuable old accustomed licensed public house occupied by Charles Bloor. The Golden

Above and opposite: Former Golden Ball public house, 2019.

Ball and the draper's shop next to it were said to be situated in and have a commanding frontage to 'one of the best thoroughfares in Newcastle' and the pub then incorporated a spacious bar, two parlours, a good kitchen and stabling and piggeries to the rear.

John Wedgwood of Burslem took on the Golden Ball in 1872, and after it had been closed for alterations, opened the hostelry as a wine and spirit vaults, offering a choice of ale, wine and spirits.

The demise of the pub came in 1936 following a meeting of the Newcastle Borough Council licensing justices: 'Mr. W. H. Abberley, applying for the transfer of the full licence of the Golden Ball to the Pool Dam Inn, said the latter was a recently erected house which, however, possessed only a beer "on" licence. The Golden Ball was situated in a crowded part of the town where public improvements were desired, and no hardship would be caused to the public by the removal ...' The licence was duly transferred.

The premises, whose Bridge Street address was later changed to High Street, became occupied by a succession of shops. It has been recognised by the Civic Society as the only timber-framed building in the town to have retained something like its original appearance.

3. Former St Giles' Rectory, Ironmarket, 1698

The building now known as Rectory Chambers needs to be considered in the context of the surrounding area.

The land on which Queen's Gardens were laid out fringed the old Coleshull Lake – the present Nelson Place area. The lake had existed since medieval times.

Much of this area was occupied by a large area of wasteland called The Marsh – indicated on a plan of the town of *c.* 1785. The present Merrial Street was once known as Marsh Street and at the top end of the town is Marsh Parade.

The Marsh occupied around 23 acres of land by this time. It became a town dumping ground for multifarious rubbish and therefore became a health hazard. It later became enclosed and was redeveloped by a body of trustees by Acts of

Below and opposite: Former St Giles' Rectory, now shops, 2019.

Parliament in 1782 and 1783. They had powers to offer building leases and soon afterwards Nelson Place, King Street, Queen Street, Brunswick Street and others were laid out.

The 1877 OS map shows a very large field next to the rectory at the foot of Ironmarket.

The rectory was attached to St Giles' Church. Its origins go back to 1698, when Sir John Leveson-Gower granted a plot of land at the east end of the street for the benefit of the then curate of Newcastle and his successors. Its first occupant was Revd Egerton Harding (d. 1717). The date of 1854 on the present building refers to the time when the property, then known as the rectory and Glebe House, was extended and enlarged by one story by Revd Veale. In 1910 it was completely restored. By 1926 it had become unmanageable as a rectory and so the site was sold, with a new rectory built in Seabridge Road. The rectory became a medical centre before being converted to retail use.

The land for the gardens, formerly glebeland and known as the Rectory Field, was purchased for £750 by public subscription and vested in the old Newcastle Corporation in 1897, the year that saw Queen Victoria's Diamond Jubilee being celebrated – hence the name of the gardens that came to be laid out on this land.

4. Former Wine Vaults Public House, High Street, Pre-1700

Elements of this listed timber-framed building date back to before 1700, though it underwent much structural alteration in its long life as a public house.

In 1835, John Shubotham announced in the local press that he had left the George & Dragon in Ironmarket and purchased the Wine & Spirit Vaults in Red Lion Square, previously occupied by wine and spirit merchant John Wilson from 1818 at the latest. Shubotham became Mayor of Newcastle-under-Lyme but died in office in 1849.

The pub was run by the Beeston family for much of the second half of the nineteenth century and the name of Beeston's Vaults was still used by Newcastle people long after the family's departure.

The booklet *Real Ale In and Around the Potteries* (1984), published by CAMRA's Potteries branch, noted: 'Outside, over archway, is remaining half of a stabling sign, offering "Good Stabling".'

The pub saw many changes in more recent times as it strove to reinvent itself. In 1996, it became O'Neill's, one of three Irish-theme pubs in the town. From a conservation point of view, there is relatively little that local authorities can do in the case of a brewery's decision to rebrand a much-loved town pub. However, Bass

Former Wine Vaults pub, 2019.

Lymestone Vaults pub, 2019.

intended more than a renaming, as reported in *The Sentinel* in December 1996, and the plans fell foul of Newcastle Borough Council. A Bass spokesman said that blue and yellow were the brand colours of the O'Neill's outlets and had been painted on seventy such outlets nationwide. The bright colour scheme was turned down by the council, which was anxious to avoid glaring colours in a conservation area.

The name of the Wine Vaults was restored in 2000. Other names such as On the Square (from May 2003) and the extremely contrived Bedd Bar (Bedd standing for Bar, Eat, Drink, Dance) signified efforts to attract a fickle pub-going public through trendy-sounding names.

The front part of the pub is now an estate agents while the Lymestone Vaults, opened by the Lymestone brewery of Stone and accessed via Pepper Street, was opened in 2012.

5. Brick Façade of the Former Pomona Works, Lower Street, c. 1700

The brick façade of the former Pomona Works is dated by Newcastle Civic Society as c. 1700. This is one of the most important archaeological locations in Newcastle owing to its importance as an early site for pottery manufacture.

Above: Maxims Nightclub, 1994.

Below: Belong, 2019.

Notes by medieval historian Thomas Pape, published in the *Evening Sentinel* newspaper in 1935, refer to a collection of eighteenth-century pottery found in 1898 nearly 6 feet below the rear of what was then the Pomona Inn (formerly the Ropers Arms). The items were mainly glazed and unglazed red and red-brown teapots.

Pape then proceeds to describe the early development of the site, referring to documents at the Public Record Office in London. An outline history can be traced back to 1655 when Elizabeth Bagnall, a widow, and Edward Bagnall, gentleman and her son, sold a house in Lower Street for £34 to John Wood. However, it is sufficient here to mention the period from 1724 to 1744 when Samuel Bell was the owner of the two houses in Lower Street. He established a potworks. Bell died in 1744, but a newspaper cutting dated 1746, sourced by Pape from the William Salt Library, reveals that John Bell let the house to William Steers, a Londoner. However, John wanted a potter to rent the whole premises. Pape quotes the newspaper notice, which advertised the property as: 'a very commodious house (late in the occupation of Mr. Bell and now in the possession of Mr. Steers), with three parlours, a hall and two kitchens ... a large garden ... sundry warehouses, workshops, lathes, throwing wheels and other utensils, useful in making fine earthenware or china.' Another potter, Joseph Wilson, came to manufacture on site.

Assessing the significance of this location, Pape wrote in 1935: 'There are records of other pot-works in Newcastle-under-Lyme, but not nearly so complete as those recording the career of Samuel Bell, gentleman, potter and Capital Burgess of the old borough.'

Further archaeological evidence about the site was gleaned in 1969–71. The building became a nightclub but in recent years has been transformed into a care home for the elderly under the name of Belong.

6. Guildhall, High Street, *c.* 1713

An earlier municipal building that was the meeting place of the Newcastle Guild Merchant was replaced by the present Guildhall shortly after 1713. John Briggs noted in *Newcastle-under-Lyme 1173–1973* that it was 'probably the first building constructed with bricks from the corporation brickyard'. Sometimes referred to as the town hall, it was described in White's Directory of 1851 as being 'raised on columns and arches, so as to form a covered market underneath'. There were alterations in 1860–61, when a magistrates' court, a grand jury room and a retiring room were incorporated on the ground floor, the upper storey being used as an assembly room. A substantial portico surmounted by a clock tower was also added. The clock was presented to the town by James Astley Hall, J.P., a former mayor.

As the focal point of the town, the Guildhall accommodated multifarious events and celebrations including billiard matches, theatrical performances and cage bird shows.

From the 1990s the question from a conservation point of view has been how to preserve and protect a building that had all but served its original purpose.

Left and below: Guildhall, 2018.

It was described as 'shabby' in 1993 when operating as a community centre, meeting room and a venue for selling goods. In 1996, the under-used Guildhall was put up for lease by its owners, Newcastle Borough Council, following renovation and repair work. More than a dozen community groups were asked to quit the premises in early 1997, and in 1999 pub chain Regent Inns were permitted to transform the building into a café bar. Faced with complaints that the chain's original choice of name – Two Halves at the Guildhall – cheapened the building, the new outlet was named, simply, the Guildhall. However, the initiative failed, and by early 2005 the building was derelict and deteriorating again.

In 2008, the building reopened as a Newcastle Borough Council customer service centre following a £1.2 million refurbishment of the Grade II listed building and the restoration of a Minton tiled floor. It closed following the relocation of staff to Castle House, but in December 2018 it was announced that Support Staffordshire would run the Guildhall as a community hub.

7. Unitarian Meeting House, off Church Street, 1717

In close proximity to St Giles' Church is the Unitarian Meeting House – the oldest Nonconformist place of worship in Newcastle – built in its original form in 1694. Its particular location and its turbulent history make it a building of note.

Unitarian Chapel, 2018.

Unitarian Chapel plaque, 2018.

Historically, the relationship between the two places of worship has been variegated, to say the least. In the seventeenth century, Revd George Long was a curate at St Giles' but left in order to preach for the dissenters.

The footpaths through St Giles' churchyard permitted access to services at the Meeting House, which might suggest an amicable relationship between the dissenters and the Anglicans. However, this was not always so. Many Anglicans couldn't help but feel provoked by the sight of leading townsmen passing through their churchyard en route to the dissenters' chapel.

In July 1715, the chapel was burnt down by a mob – with the churchwardens of St Giles' playing a part in the destruction.

However, the Unitarians were nothing if not determined, and they rebuilt their chapel in 1717, funded by compensation awarded by the subsequent court case.

The building's connections with several notable individuals also add to its importance. Records prove that Dr Joseph Priestley (1733–1804), the renowned chemist who isolated oxygen, conducted worship here around 1761 while he was Unitarian minister at Nantwich in Cheshire. Intriguing emphasis on the connection of the Potteries industrialist Josiah Wedgwood with neighbouring Newcastle-under-Lyme is shown by the fact that he and his family not only worshipped here but played a leading role in the running of the chapel. His brother-in-law, William Willetts, was minister between 1727 and 1776, afterwards being succeeded by his son.

In 1926, an upper extension was added in order to provide space for a schoolroom, and the front of the building rendered in order to conceal the contrasting bricks.

Old photographs show the cluster of buildings that surrounded the chapel, but slum clearance and the arrival of a town bypass in the 1960s effectively made the chapel considerably more visible to those travelling through Newcastle.

8. Former Newcastle Conservative Club, Merrial Street, 1769

The *Victoria County History* refers to a house, the Hawthorns, in Merrial Street, of 1769 that had been occupied since *c.* 1874 by the Conservative Club, together with a slightly later house adjoining it.

Above and below: Former Conservative Club, 2019.

Further information can be found in the Historical Record of Events and Personalities of the Newcastle-under-Lyme Conservative Club (1968), formerly held at Newcastle Reference Library.

The record dates the building at between 1727 and 1760 and conveys that the property was originally two dwelling houses: Wilton House, occupied by Samuel Wilton, who was described as a joiner, and Hawthorne House, occupied by a Josiah Wedgwood. The date given for the formation of the club is 1868, its first meeting being on 18 December that year. Robert Heath JP was the first president, remaining in the position until his death in 1893. In 1874 and 'in consequence of a feeling of insecurity of tenure of the premises now occupied by the Club', the members formed a limited company and purchased the premises from Wilton, becoming the proprietors of what were then known as the Carlton and Hawthorne Houses, which they ultimately converted into club premises.

In 1890, the front grounds of the club, which had hitherto been untidy, were laid out, painted and fenced and in 1901 a skittle alley was laid down, which proved so successful that a pavilion was subsequently added. This was swiftly made available for concerts, whist drives and socials. The club's annual report for 1903 reveals that a miniature rifle range had proved a successful amenity and this was brought into requisition with the outbreak of the First World War. In August 1914, it was announced that there would be shooting instruction at the club in response to Lord Kitchener's suggestion that rifle clubs' facilities should be used by young men and youths willing to learn to use a rifle. Reference was made to the 'admirable range in the skittle pavilion of the club'.

Pevsner (1974) described the premises as a five-bay rendered house with a doorway with broken pediment on Tuscan columns. He also referred to the date of 1769 on a rainwater head.

9. The Polite Vicar Pub and Restaurant, Etruria Road, *c.* 1782

This property, on what was known as the Stoneyfields Estate, was a Georgian house of some importance. It was built *c.* 1782 for the Hatrell family, with this date appearing on a downspout on the front of the building that survived for many years. A plan of Newcastle-under-Lyme dated *c.* 1785 indicates 'Mrs Hatrell's house' on the road to Etruria.

At various times it was the home of many enterprising individuals in Newcastle and the Potteries including the Bent family, Nigel Heathcote, and the ironmaster Thomas Firmstone.

A *Staffordshire Mercury* press notice announcing the sale of 'Stony Field' in 1835 advertised some of the property's home comforts including a nearly new semi-grand pianoforte, handsome lamps, plated articles and the neatly bound Britanica Encyclopaedia all belonging to Heathcote, who intended to move elsewhere.

In the 1920s the house was bought by well-known local surgeon Dr Eric Young. After his death the house fell into disrepair and decay. However, when historian

Above: Polite Vicar, 1998.

Below: Polite Vicar, 2019.

Ernest Warrillow took photographs of the house in 1956 and 1963, he wrote that it was in beautiful condition and surrounded by trees. He wrote that it stood a good chance of 'surviving for many years'. That it did was due to the fact that it became used as offices. It served as offices even in Warrillow's time and was bought by Morgan Insurance in 1967, formally opening as their offices in February 1969.

Following its period of being occupied by Morgan Insurance, the building was converted by Tom Cobleigh plc into a pub/restaurant called the Polite Vicar, officially opening in 1997. The eponymous 'Polite Vicar' was Revd Ian Gregory, minister of King Street Congregational Church and founder of the Polite Society. At the time when mansion was being converted into a restaurant, Revd Gregory told *The Sentinel* that there were reasons why some people didn't go to church and that the public house was the next best thing. He even added that Jesus Christ would find himself just as at home in a good pub as he would in a church.

10. Former Mic House, Queen Street, c. 1785

Last used as offices called Mic House, this property now stands derelict almost opposite St George's Church.

What was originally a three-storey residence was erected on land leased from the Marsh Trustees and designed by John Pepper. Its extension, to its left, was built by Thomas Mayer between 1812 and 1815.

Below and opposite: Former Mic House, 2019.

Pepper, who was a builder and architect, lived at No. 2 Queen Street, until his death in 1811. Its central doorway makes it particularly notable. There is a classical surround that encompasses a medallion, above the door, depicting a cherub and a lion.

Pepper made a major contribution to the building of Georgian Newcastle. He laid out Pepper Street, running alongside the present Butters John Bee estate agents off Red Lion Square and he also designed the Newcastle and Pottery Theatre at the foot of King Street – afterwards a cinema and demolished in 1963.

A document in the Staffordshire Record Office relating to the repairs of St Giles' in Newcastle-under-Lyme in 1796 confirms an agreement between the church officials, Matthew Fishwick (plasterer) and John Pepper (architect).

John Pepper's memorial can be found in St Giles' churchyard.

11. Former Lace Gentlemen's Club, Ironmarket, *c.* 1790

The former Compasses Inn became the Crossways in 1974. Following a lengthy period of closure in 2002–03, a small business group, Rippins Ltd, proposed to paint the building pink and reopen it as the Corner House.

Above: Compasses Inn, overlooking Nelson Place.

Below: Former Lace Gentlemen's Club, 2019.

However, several people contacted *The Sentinel* newspaper to comment on the plans and objected to the pink colour scheme with the result that light green was ultimately chosen. It reopened as the Queen Victoria in September 2003 in acknowledgment of the statue of the former monarch in Queen's Gardens opposite.

The new pub was visited by *Sentinel* journalist Kerryanne Clancy, who commented on the refurbished interior: 'Certainly a sunny yellow lick of paint inside has given the pub a modern cheery look and the light solid pine tables and chairs in all shapes and sizes around the room wouldn't look out of place at Habitat.'

Rippins' stated objective was to target the older drinking market, though Kerryanne mused that the Queen Victoria might prove too old for the young and too young for the old.

However, this prime site building again became derelict prior to taking on a new identity as the Lace Gentlemen's Club, a lap dancing venue that opened in 2007. It was a controversial initiative that drew comments from many quarters prior to opening. Simon Tagg, the Conservative leader of the council, questioned whether it was really the direction that Newcastle wished to take – citing objections from the police. There were also objections from religious bodies and the Hanley-based Women's Rape and Sexual Violence Service, though entrepreneur Mo Chowdry, who had owned the Queen Victoria, had replied in *The Sentinel*: 'Let the market determine whether this is right rather than a bunch of church-goers and charities.'

He added that the building had never worked as a pub, though this might be disputed by those who imbibed at the busy Crossways in the mid-1990s when a house beer, Bear Cross Bitter, was sold for a hugely generous 99p a pint.

At the time of writing the building has been derelict for some time.

12. Former Castle Hotel Frontage (in part), High Street, c. 1820

The Castle Hotel opened around 1820, and although the original building may have been older, the hotel belongs to what might be described as the twilight days of the coaching era in Newcastle.

In the nineteenth century, celebration dinners at the Castle Hotel accommodated people of wealth and status such as civic dignitaries.

Trust Houses Ltd took over the hotel in 1935, and it became an extremely noted and well-advertised music and dance venue – especially on Saturday evenings when bands played for the crowds.

Some of the reasons for the ultimate closure of the hotel are explained in a later chapter. The threat to the building's future – and a planning application for a three-storey supermarket building to replace it – triggered the establishment of

Newcastle Civic Society, whose chairman, B. J. Browning, wrote to the *Evening Sentinel* in May 1968:

> My Committee feel that some public protest should be made against the spoliation of such a central site and the loss of a building of such character and architectural merit to the heart of the town. That such wanton destruction of this fine old town should continue without protest from its citizens is the reason for the coming into existence of the Newcastle-under-Lyme Civic Society of which I have the honour to be Chairman.

However, the hotel closed and a sale of its furniture and effects took place in the yard and the old ballroom in June 1968. The building remained intact until 1969 when Tesco Ltd incorporated their new premises into it. This development occurred despite a campaign and a 6,000-name petition to save the Castle Hotel. Ultimately, a decision was made to preserve part of the Georgian façade, with Len Daniels, the Secretary of the Newcastle Civic Society, commenting in 1970 that 'It must be understood it was our intention to save the whole hotel but failing this we felt that there was a need to preserve the façade as we felt this was related to the surrounding property and we were afraid the new building would not be in character with the surrounding buildings.'

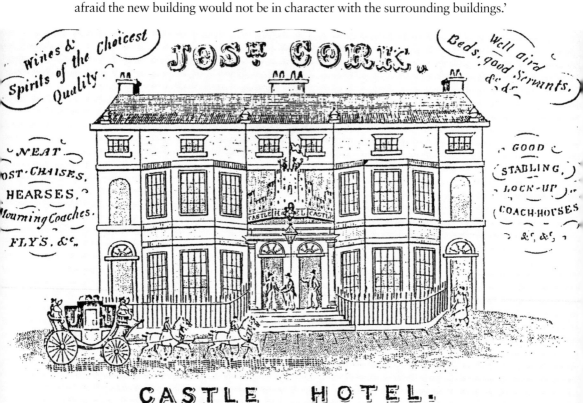

Castle Hotel advertisement from a trade directory, 1839.

Former Castle Hotel frontage, 2019.

13. Higherland Methodist Church, Higherland, 1823 (with additions)

This building was originally a Primitive Methodist chapel, reminding us of the ideological divisions that grew within the Methodist movement. Primitive Methodism was instigated in North Staffordshire around 1810. The movement's chapels were architecturally fairly plain, reflecting the low church worship practised by its adherents. Significantly, a report of Edward Wilson, senior physician to the North Staffordshire Infirmary, referring to the prevalence of cholera in 1847, stated: 'As seats of excessive morality, I should name the Upper and Lower Greens, Fletcher-street, Holborn, Lower-street, Pool Dam, Goose-street, and the alleys opening into those streets, and indeed, the whole of the lower parts of the town, and the Higher Land.' The cholera map of 1849 indicates that several cases of cholera occurred adjacent the chapel.

The chapel at Higherland contrasts starkly with the magnificence of the building erected by the affluent Methodist New Connexion in Newcastle in 1858, which is featured in a later chapter.

The original congregation would have met at each other's houses, but they decided to build a place of worship at Higherland. The foundation stone of 1823

Above: Methodist Church at Higherland, 1995.

Below: Methodist Church at Higherland, 2019.

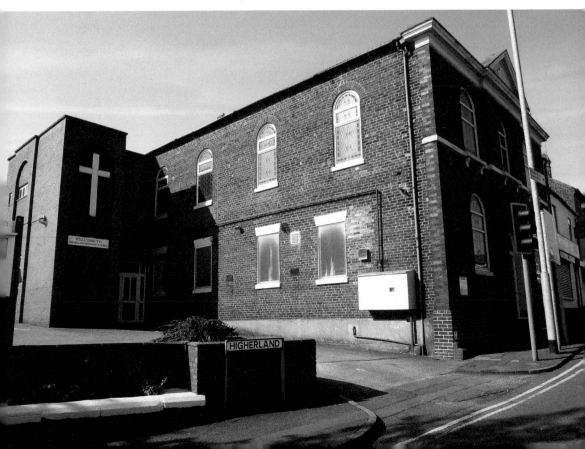

is to be found in the present vestry. The building was not registered as a place of worship until 1828, with baptismal records beginning in 1845.

A Sunday school was required and a stone commemorating its addition can be seen on the outside wall of the old premises to the rear, bearing the date of 1836. It is assumed that the first church had only one storey, but a major addition was made in 1853 – a date that appears in the pediment of the present building.

Following a major refurbishment in 1897, there were reopening services in March 1898. The schoolroom section was also extended around this period.

From the late 1980s major improvements and renovations were made. A final service took place in the 'old' chapel on 28 February 1993. The alterations saw a new place of worship being established at first-floor level, with a coffee lounge and activity rooms on the ground floor.

I am indebted to Peter Butler and Elizabeth Longshaw for much of the information in this chapter.

14. St George's Church, Queen Street, 1828

This was a Commissioners' Anglican church, financed from a national fund that had been set up by the government to establish places of worship in growing urban areas. It effectively reduced accommodation pressures on St Giles' Church, being a chapel of ease, and ultimately becoming the head of its own parish in 1844.

In 1826, Newcastle Corporation sold the commissioners a parcel of land called the Cherry Orchard in The Brampton.

The architect was Francis Bedford of London and the builder was Sant of Burslem. Consecrated in 1828, it was built in the Gothic style of architecture and able to accommodate over 1,500 persons. There were extensive alterations in 1879–81 and a new north-west porch was added in 1928.

The church was sited on part of The Marsh estate, on rising ground, and was 124 feet in length from east to west, being 67 feet from north to south. The outer walls were supported by buttresses surmounted by richly carved pinnacles 11 feet in height in the style of the fourteenth century. The west tower incorporated battlements and pinnacles.

It was constructed from stone taken from Chapel Chorlton quarry. This stone was described at the time: 'Though inferior in beauty to some others – in that most essential quality of durability, [it] is not exceeded by any stone in this county, granite only excepted.'

As Newcastle Civic Society pointed out in its *Town Portrait* of 1984, Bedford's churches 'seem to have suffered due to the pressure of work at this time, but St George's has survived without major repair until the last few years when cleaning and renewal of perished stonework was undertaken'.

However, in 1990, *The Sentinel* reported on the consequences of the 'building blunder' of 162 years previous: 'Workmen putting up the structure in 1828 fitted

Above and below: St George's Church, 2019.

stone cladding to the outside of the church the wrong way around. This caused the normal weathering process to speed up.'

Cholera victims were buried in the churchyards of both St Giles' and St George's, while 'a day of humiliation and prayer' – held in consequence of the spread of the pernicious disease – was marked by service at both churches in August 1832.

15. Holy Trinity Church, London Road, 1834

Holy Trinity was one of the first Catholic churches to be erected following the granting of freedom of worship in 1829.

Like No. 1 London Road standing almost opposite, this Roman Catholic church building has always excited comment.

Its opening was described without much of a fanfare in the *North Staffordshire Mercury* in May 1834, though the newspaper did describe it as 'one of the most splendid places of worship, unconnected with the Establishment, to be found in this county'. Revd James Egan, the then resident priest, designed the building and also furnished designs for the moulds used in making the bricks.

Many authorities endeavoured to describe its architecture, with Keates' Gazetteer and Directory of 1892–93 referring to its 'peculiar Gothic structure which many persons greatly admire'. It referred to the façade, mainly constructed

Holy Trinity Church, 1994.

Holy Trinity Church interior, showing a wedding ceremony in 1959.

from vitrified bricks, having 'the appearance of cast metal' and being relieved by quatrefoils and other devices. Also mentioned were the window frames, 'mostly of cast iron, rich in Gothic tracery'.

Pevsner, writing in his *Buildings of England: Staffordshire* (1974) was similarly intrigued, noting that Revd Egan 'was not a connoisseur of the Gothic style, but he had the right ideas and created a church which one will always remember, and with an affectionate smile. The whole façade is faced with dark blue bricks, and over the whole façade tier upon tier of blank arcading is distributed. Just one window with intersecting tracery built up of bricks. The nave top is flat and embattled, the aisle tops are lower and flat and embattled. The interior is idiosyncratic too.'

There were alterations following the appointment of Father Maguire in 1879 and again in 1930. The church is Grade II listed.

Of all the comments that have been offered on the architecture of Holy Trinity, the one that pleases the most comes from Pevsner. It could easily be missed, as it appears in a footnote in the introduction to his Staffordshire volume: 'Egan's Catholic church at Newcastle of 1833–4 ... looks roguish too, but the reason here is probably blissful ignorance rather than deliberate perversity.'

16. Former Orme School, Orme Road, 1851

Opened in 1851, the Orme English School was erected by the trustees of the late Revd Edward Orme's charity on a site formerly occupied by the town's workhouse. It was constructed of local sandstone by Messrs Byrne of Stoke

Above and below: Orme Centre, 2019.

and designed by Henry Ward of Hanley in the Elizabethan style of architecture. It incorporated castellated parapets and mullioned windows, and in its architectural style stood comparison with Newcastle's 1850s Covered Market building, which was demolished in 1961. However, later alterations have robbed the building of some of its original ornamentation. The *Staffordshire Advertiser* reported that the building 'comprises a lofty, spacious, and well-lighted and ventilated school-room, with a comfortable house adjoining for the master, all of stone'.

Its first master was Emmanuel Earl, who had previously made a success of running the local British School, erected in 1834. He was paid a salary of £120 a year plus the house, coal and attached garden.

The new school proposed to offer 'a good education, free of charge, to a considerable number of boys, the children of the middle and lower classes of the inhabitants'.

One of those boys was Arnold Bennett, the future *Five Towns* novelist, who was admitted on 9 May 1882. A plaque inside the present building commemorating the Bennett connection was unveiled in 2005.

Between 1872 and 1907 this seat of learning operated as Orme Middle School and then as Orme Boys School between 1907 and 1928. The school was roundly condemned by the Education Board inspectors in 1923, and from 1928 it reopened on an all-new site as Wolstanton County Grammar School.

In 1931, the Orme Road building was bought by Newcastle Education Committee and reopened as Orme Boys Senior School, taking pupils from Hassall Street and Ryecroft. It became a county secondary school after 1944.

In more recent years, the former Orme School was reinvented as the Poolfields Youth and Community Centre and then the Orme Centre. By March 1991 it was accommodating twenty adult education classes, three youth clubs and North Staffordshire's only handicapped playgroup, being regularly used by around 600 people a week.

17. Pitfield House, Brampton Park, c. 1854

Pitfield House was built in the mid-1850s for Henry Hall, who was a timber merchant operating in Nelson Place. He became prosperous and was able to build this two-story brick villa residence. Like many prominent traders in Newcastle, he was involved in civic affairs, serving on the town council. He served as an alderman and was mayor in 1842–43. He died in 1871 and was buried in the family vault in St George's Church. However, his wife continued to live at Pitfield House until the 1870s when it was bought by Stephen Edge, a corn merchant, who moved the short distance from The Firs. It remained in private ownership until being bought by Newcastle Council in 1939, after which date the council

Above and below: Pitfield House, 2018.

opened up Pitfield House to the public as well as its extensive grounds. In recent years, Pitfield House served as a venue for arts and education, with Newcastle Players, Relate and Newcastle Play Council – which organised play schemes for children – all using the house at various times. This surviving and very elegant structure serves as a reminder of the progress being made by affluent tradesmen and merchants in early Victorian Newcastle.

18. The Firs, Brampton Park, 1855

The Firs was built in 1854–55 for Thomas Leech, who was a cheese factor, maltster and skinner. This villa-style house incorporates broken pediments, impressive dentils below roof level, attractive brickwork and quoins (dressed stones at the angles of the building).

The house came to be associated with the Moseley family. The Moseley Brothers, whose general drapers was established in 1851, stocked an extensive range of clothing in their premises in High Street. They owned two of the twenty-four drapers in the town in 1865 and one of the five that remained in 1893. The Moseleys became involved in local politics, with Ralph becoming Mayor of Newcastle-under-Lyme in 1866, whilse he was a councillor for the town on many occasions.

Ralph bought The Firs for the sum of £3,400 in 1863. There is an excellent surviving photo of a wedding party standing in front of The Firs on 12 August 1891. This was the marriage of Richard Bartlett Mellard and Beatrice Mosley, whose family occupied the house. Both families were well-known traders in High Street, Newcastle, the Mellards being ironmongers. In 1955, The Firs and its surrounding land (3 acres and 26.5 perches) were sold to Newcastle Borough Council for £6,325.

From 1956 the property came to accommodate Newcastle Borough Museum and Art Gallery, which houses Chinese pottery, Staffordshire chimney ornaments, circus figures, a display of clay pipes, John Smith's iron gravestone (transferred from St Giles' Church) and the bust of Horatio Nelson that formerly stood in the pediment of the old Borough Treasurer's offices in Nelson Place.

There is also a social history gallery depicting shop premises including Mellard's the ironmongers, a pawn shop, a chemist's and a doctor's surgery.

Larger items include the pub sign from the demolished Smithfield pub in Lower Street and the Wrinehill Upper Gate tollgate sign of *c.* 1830. The clock mechanism, donated by Edward Turner, a local chemist and druggist, and installed in the Municipal Hall in 1890, was later removed to Newcastle Library but in April 2018 was rehoused in the museum.

The Crimean War cannon was removed to its present site outside the museum in 1965.

Above: Borough Museum and Art Gallery, 2018.

Right: Borough Museum and Art Gallery detail, 2018.

19. Militia Barracks, Barracks Road, 1855

The attractive, red-brick, Italianate façade incorporates stone dressings and a central projecting entrance embracing a round-arched doorway and turret above. The windows have stone mullions. The buildings behind overlook four sides of a courtyard.

Until 1880 the barracks served as the headquarters of the 3rd King's Own Staffordshire Rifle Regiment, which met annually at Newcastle for training. The year 1882 saw the barracks being purchased by W. H. Dalton, a major in the Staffordshire Rangers Volunteers. A trust oversaw the use of the buildings for the Rifle Volunteers of Newcastle. The Volunteers were replaced by the Territorials in 1907, with the corporation becoming trustees of the barracks in 1925.

Alderman A. Ryles, writing in *A Positive Page* (1977), wrote that the Territorials paid £50 per annum to the North Staffordshire Regiment, which terminated in 1938 when the Territorial Buildings at Cross Heath were completed. The Territorials vacated the barracks in 1937 and during the Second World War they were used as the headquarters of the Ambulance Section in Civil Defence, with men and women being trained in first aid.

In 1952, the Barracks Trust was established, allowing the Territorials to use the building as and when required. Otherwise it was to be used or let by the corporation for the benefit of the borough.

Below and opposite: Former Barracks, 2019.

Ryles also wrote of what became an important function of the barracks:

An opportunity arose to use the Barracks at one of the Labour Exchange Advisory Committee meetings when one of the regional officers came, and he with us regretted that we had over 80 cases of unemployed disabled people. He indicated that if premises were available he would have a section of Remploy in Newcastle. I begged permission to show him the facilities of the Barracks, and we obtained a tenancy for 20 odd to commence a book-binding service and as space became available the numbers increased over the 23 years to nearly 80. The accommodation was poor but it was a good start.

These workers were subsequently housed in a factory in the Lyme Valley.

The Barracks Trust, the charitable company that owns the building, rents out its units to local businesses and charities.

20. Former Ebenezer Chapel, Ryecroft, 1858

On New Year's Day 1856, a public tea party was held in the Ebenezer Chapel schoolroom, followed by a public meeting in the chapel itself. This highlighted the plans for a new chapel about to be erected, and indeed, a beautiful transparency plan, showing the front elevation of the new building, was displayed.

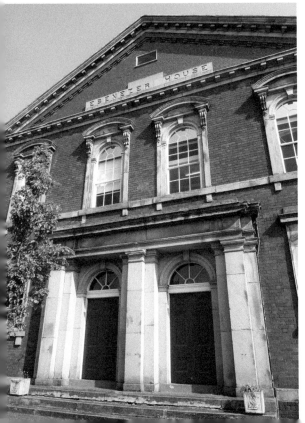

Above and left: Former Ebenezer Church, 2018.

Ebenezer Chapel replaced the earlier Methodist New Connexion chapel located in nearby Marsh Street (later Merrial Street). It cost nearly £3,000. It was a magnificent expression of Nonconformist affluence at the time of its opening in April 1858, as was emphasised by a splendid drawing by Buckler.

The opening was marred by the type of incident that underlined the need for religion as a controlling force in Newcastle. At the conclusion of the evening services on the Sabbath, the congregation exited only to find themselves jostled and crushed by a gang of young thieves. Many had their pockets picked, and one lady, it was reported, 'lost £8, which she had placed in her pocket for safety, in case thieves should break into her house while she was in attendance' at the chapel.

It was a two-storey construction in the classical style incorporating a stone portico and a handsome pediment. It was built from Sandon red brick with stone dressings and copings. The interior could accommodate between 900 and 1,000 worshippers and had a beautifully panelled ceiling. The architect was J. Simpson of Leeds and the building contractor Mr. R. Chapman of Newcastle. It was envisaged upon opening that the grounds would be planted with shrubs and trees and fenced by palisades.

A manse – a house provided for the minister of certain Christian churches – was built on the west side of the chapel in 1869.

In 1872, Ebenezer became the head of the newly formed Newcastle Circuit. In 1897 its designation was altered to Ebenezer Church.

In 1981 the chapel closed and the building, renamed Ebenezer House, has since been used for retail and office accommodation. The building was Grade II listed in 1972.

21. Congregational Chapel, King Street, 1859

The Congregationalist cause was said to have been begun in Newcastle in 1779. The Congregational chapel was erected on the site of an older chapel designated the Marsh Chapel. Having been built in 1784, it had fallen into a state of dilapidation and had become too small for a growing congregation.

At the time of the foundation stone laying of the new chapel, sermons were preached in the new Methodist New Connexion chapel in Merrial Street, and 'Friends and members of other religious denominations' were kindly invited to unite with the congregation for the services. This spirit of denominational flexibility was promoted at the opening service of the new chapel, when it was claimed that 'the denominationalism in Christian Churches was the child of noble parentage and had effected much good … notwithstanding the apparent diversities of opinion'.

The building's architectural style is Gothic, of the Decorated period. Its exterior architecture was described in detail upon the chapel's opening in 1859, and though alterations have since been made in regard to its frontal access, the quirky charm of this edifice is still observable today.

The front was then enclosed with massive stone buttresses, iron rails and sliding gates with a flight of steps approaching the triple arched porch, which incorporated handsome capitals. The large rose window was – and still is – the outstanding feature. At the angle of the building was an octagon tower and spire rising to 90 feet. Also notable was the ornamental brick facing, juxtaposing yellow brick with bands of blue brick at regular intervals. When first built, the colour contrast must have been stunning. Dressings of Hollington stone were also incorporated. The windows were glazed throughout with rough quarry glass.

Internally, iron columns with twisted shafts and moulded and gilt capitals supported the arches. A schoolroom occupied the whole of the area under the chapel and this was able to accommodate between 350 and 400 children.

The builder was John Pooley of Peterborough, the architect being R. Moffat Smith of Manchester.

The church was restored in 1990, becoming a listed building the year after.

Congregational Church entrance, 2019.

Congregational Church from the rear, 2019.

22. St Giles' Church, Church Lane, 1876

St Giles' Church dates back to the twelfth century and was formerly dependent on Trentham Priory, but from the thirteenth century was subordinate to the church at Stoke as a chapel of ease. It would remain so until 1807 when it became a separate parish.

The base of the church tower dates back to the thirteenth century, though there is disagreement on how many churches have been attached to it. The present one was said to have been the fourth when the new church was opened in 1876.

The church of 1721 was, by the early 1870s, in a dilapidated condition, with the architect Sir George Gilbert Scott (1811–78) being approached to replace it. He stated:

The Tower alone remains of the Ancient Church. This is a vast and originally a noble structure, still structurally strong, though externally sadly decayed. This is, in its lower parts, of the 13th century. Its middle stages are of the 14th, and some parts of a somewhat later date. It is probable that the Church destroyed about 1720 was of a corresponding character, and that the whole formed a noble

Above: St Giles' Church, 2018.

Left: St Giles' Church doorway, 2018.

edifice. At that date, however, the Church was rebuilt as we now see it, in a character bearing no resemblance to the original Church, or to the ancient tower to which it is attached. I need hardly offer any remarks on the existing structure. It speaks for itself; a plain brick building without, and in a style more like a Town Hall than a Church.

Scott was a Gothic revivalist, as is evident in his earlier Holy Trinity Church, Hartshill (1842). He was heavily influenced by Pugin, who believed that Gothic architecture of medieval times most represented the high ideals of the supposed golden age of the Christian Church.

Scott's new St Giles' was designed in the thirteenth-century style, harmonising with the tower.

The 110-foot tower remains a prominent landmark, despite there being no spire. Its ground floor is thirteenth century and it incorporates lancet windows.

The tower was restored and refaced in 1894. The original fine pinnacles were supplanted by the crocketted pinnacles that we see today.

23. Wall and Archway, Ryecroft/Queen Street, 1886

This substantial structure remains an ornament to the town and merits inclusion in this book.

Its date refers to the completion of the churchyard improvements that took place from 1885 to 1886. It was erected by prosperous local builder John Gallimore.

By this date, Newcastle's Municipal Cemetery of 1866 had long been established, helping to ease pressing issues over the scarcity of burial space in town.

Interments at St George's churchyard were discontinued in June 1866 except in certain graves.

In November 1885, it was announced that a bazaar would be held as a fundraiser for the churchyard improvements.

It was supported by Newcastle's mayor and corporation, and numerous influential individuals including the Duke and Duchess of Sutherland, Captain Edwards-Heathcote, industrialist Francis Stanier and Potteries philanthropist Smith Child.

There was a growing feeling in Newcastle – as in the Potteries – that graveyards in busy public places should not appear grim and unkempt in serving their purpose. Indeed, the *Staffordshire Advertiser* remarked in 1885 that town graveyards might even beautify the towns they served: 'In large centres of population, the beautifully-kept cemetery is frequently the one bright spot of a crowded town … providing an attractive resort and a breathing space for the living.'

It is intriguing, considering that the recent renovation of St Giles' churchyard was feared by some as a prospective 'Disneyfication' of the grounds, that the *Staffordshire Advertiser* should champion such an enlightened view of churchyard improvements: 'Neglect and gloomy associations are no longer characteristics of

Left: St George's churchyard entrance, 1996.

Below: St George's churchyard, 2019.

burial grounds, and it is certainly right and fitting that [St George's churchyard] with its fine situation and capabilities of improvement should be redeemed from the air of neglect which it has lately borne.' The newspaper added that the efforts of the vicar, churchwardens and congregation would benefit local inhabitants 'regardless of denomination'. Indeed, many donations towards the churchyard improvements came from 'liberal and unsectarian support'.

The stone gateway and perimeter wall gave emphasis to the improvements to the southern end of the churchyard, which presently contains bench seats for those who wish to enjoy peaceful surroundings or sit while waiting for their bus by the Brampton bus stop.

24. Former Bear Hotel, West Brampton, c. 1888

This fine building was opened as the flagship hotel of Ridgway's Brewery of Lower Street, but was later owned by Parker's Burslem Brewery. It was conveniently near for railway passengers, the branch line above the hotel having been opened in 1852. Newcastle-under-Lyme railway station, overlooking King Street, was also a short distance away. The hotel swiftly became a community hub, playing host to the West Brampton bowling club (it incorporated a bowling alley) and staging functions organised by the proprietors of Enderley Mills, a prominent factory nearby that specialised in army clothing. One of these events took place in early 1914, with the *Staffordshire Advertiser* reporting: 'The cutting-room staff at the Enderley Mills of Messrs. Hammond and Co. entertained the male staff of the firm's branch at Crewe to dinner at the Bear Hotel on Saturday. The visitors, numbering about 20, made an inspection of the mills and the town before sitting down to a convivial repast, presided over by Mr. W. Brealey.'

In late 1964, the Bear's Cavern Club – an attempt to cash in on the Beatles phenomenon – opened in the cellars of the building for the pleasure of what its press advertisement called 'Beat hungry teenagers'. It played host to local groups and those from further afield. It featured a bar counter in log cabin style while serving 'Double Diamond, the beer that the men drink'. As with anything else, it had to change with the times, and it reopened in August 1969 as a Continental-style cellar bar under licensee William Hulme. It later became a basement discotheque, and through several changes continued to stage live music for decades.

The hostelry could boast of a multiroomed layout that could accommodate the meetings of various groups. The Potteries branch of CAMRA held its AGM there in 2001. For some years it also played host to an informal group of elderly singers on Saturday nights. It closed in 2003.

It presently houses several flats and has adopted the name of De Brompton Court. The name is significant because William de Brompton was one of the most important burgesses of Newcastle-under-Lyme in the late fourteenth century.

Left: Bear public house's front entrance with fanlight window, 1998.

Below: Former Bear public house, now apartments, 2019.

25. Ten Green Bottles, Merrial Street, 1895

Like many late Victorian buildings, this one boasts of elegant tile and terracotta decoration in its upper frontage, below a steeply pitched roof. There are ball finials at the corner angles and the date of construction is picked out in relief above two elegant round-headed windows.

Like many retail premises in Newcastle, this building's impressive upper storey has survived intact, though its ground floor has suffered much alteration, illustrating that one of the most potent threats to the architectural quality and character of historic towns is posed by retail redevelopment.

Disagreement over such matters was noticed in 2010, when Newcastle Borough Council – supported by Newcastle Civic Society – drew up a list of sixty-four buildings and structures worthy of inclusion in a 'protected' local list, only to have the inclusion of the Roebuck Shopping Centre objected to by the owners of the centre.

In recent years, the Merrial Street building has been occupied by retailers Gulliver's and, later, Timpson's. However, since 2015 it has accommodated an upmarket micropub, Ten Green Bottles, which sells a wide range of beverages. The building remains open and successful at a time (2019) when the former Conservative Club, Civic Offices and police station in Merrial Street stand derelict.

Below left: Gulliver's shop premises, 1994.

Below right: Ten Green Bottles bar, 2019.

26. Former Ebenezer Sunday School, Merrial Street, 1898

The Methodist New Connexion Society in Newcastle was operating by September 1797 and in 1799 a chapel, named Ebenezer by 1803, was erected in Marsh Street. It was one of the oldest Sunday schools in the district. This chapel was replaced in 1858 and is described earlier.

This building's foundation stone bears the date of 25 August 1898 and was laid by Miss Tipping of Alderley Edge. Information given in *The Sentinel* newspaper at the time of the foundation stone laying offers us a useful timeline. According to records, declared the newspaper, the school was established in 1800 (hence the date at the top of the building), though it was not until three years later that it found a permanent home, when the buildings were erected. Ten years after, the premises were extended and in 1822 the schools were rebuilt. They were enlarged in 1850 but continued to grow, hence the rebuilding of 1898. However, as the press report revealed, the rebuilding embraced elements of the previous structure.

In making the alterations, the Marsh Street Lecture Hall main wall and roof were retained as well as the front elevation, though the front of the school was cemented.

Former Ebenezer Schoolrooms, 2018.

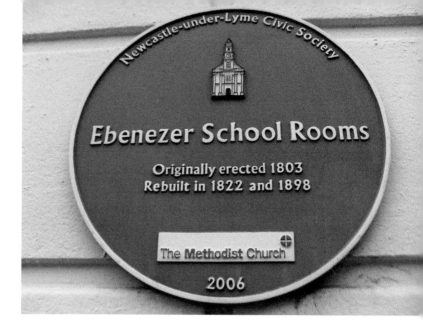

Former Ebenezer
Schoolrooms
plaque, 2015.

At the time of the foundation stone laying, Revd Bartram declared that 'the old structure had already undergone a great transformation'. The building at that time was described thus:

> A corridor seven feet wide runs the length of the building to the main staircase leading to a large assembly-room – 59 feet by 35 feet – above. From the corridor are several classrooms with accommodation for 190 boys. The girls' school has, with the exception of a portion of the front wall, been pulled down and rebuilt. There are five class-rooms on the ground floor, a large room on the upper floor, and a similar room connected by sliding doors, giving accommodation for 245 girls and infants, exclusive of the assembly-room. Thus there is accommodation for 435 children.

The architect was John Lewis of Newcastle and the contractor Mr Bagnall of Fenton.

Many community activities have taken place in the present building.

27. St Paul's Church, Victoria Road, 1908

The Church of St Paul's origins are linked to the growth of the Anglican Church in the town of Newcastle. In 1882, Revd Richard Ward, the vicar of St George's, appealed for more church accommodation in the district. A. F. Coghill duly gave a site in Victoria Road adjoining the Stubbs Walks and a temporary tin church was erected by public subscription in 1885. However, at a vestry meeting at St George's in 1905, the officers of the tin mission church urged the parish to take up the work of constructing a permanent structure for the St Paul's district, promising £1,000 towards the building fund. The new church's foundation stone

Left: St Paul's Church on a picture postcard sent in 1908.

Below: St Paul's Church, 2019.

was laid on 15 June 1905. St Paul's was constituted a separate parish on 7 August 1905 by an order in council, and the boundary of the new parish extended to Stoke workhouse, Stubbs Gate, Hassell Street, George Street and Boundary Street.

The new church was consecrated by the Bishop of Lichfield on 29 April 1908. The architects were Robert Scrivener & Sons and they designed the church in the medieval Perpendicular style. The building contractor was John Bagnall of Fenton.

The porch at the base of the tower was erected in memory of the late Revd Richard Ward, vicar of St. George's between 1875 and 1895, 'in fulfilment of whose wish this church is built to replace a temporary church wherewith he met the immediate need of a growing population, this tower and spire have been erected by A. F. Coghill.'

The local press stated that the 150-foot tower was 10 feet higher than the tower of Holy Trinity Church at Hartshill.

The aisles were paved with Minton tiles and the choir stalls were given by prominent industrialist Robert Heath of Biddulph Grange. The new church could accommodate 506 worshippers.

The total cost was nearly £5,000, exclusive of the spire and tower. A. F. Coghill gave £3,000 to the building fund as well as £3,000 to the endowment and he erected the spire and tower at a further cost of £4,500.

The church was Grade II listed in 1972.

28. Arnold Machin Pub, Ironmarket, 1914

This building has traded since 2002 as the Arnold Machin public house and is described in *Newcastle-under-Lyme Pubs* (2016) by Mervyn Edwards.

However, from 1914 the building operated as Newcastle's post office, its imminent opening being reported in the *Staffordshire Sentinel* of 26 January.

It replaced a previous post office in High Street and was erected on land bought by the government from the Ecclesiastical Commissioners. It was situated next to St Giles' Rectory and opposite the Municipal Hall.

The site had a frontage of 50 feet and a depth of 198 feet and the building was divided into three sections. Its interior contained a public office and the postmaster's office on the ground floor, a stationery storeroom, a battery room and a retiring room. Polished teak and a mahogany counter greeted the public upon entering.

The post office had already begun to prove its worth even prior to its official opening: a month before, the pressures of dealing with the mail over the busy Christmas period were addressed by utilising the sorting room – which by then had been completed – on site. This room operated highly effectively, incorporating two glass enclosures – one for the handling of registered letters and the other being used by the superintendent from which he could exercise complete supervision of

Left: Post office, 1995.

Below: Arnold Machin (Wetherspoon) pub, 2016.

the sorting department. There was even a watchroom, from where the progress of workers could be observed. Retiring rooms for the workers were fitted out with small ranges and lockers.

The post office was built of red brick with Hollington white stone facings. It was fireproof, with floors and the roof of reinforced concrete – while consideration had been given to future development. The government had also acquired a plot of land to the rear that was earmarked for the possible future erection of a telephone exchange.

The building was designed by Mr E. Cropper, architect for HM Office of Works and erected by Messrs Meiklejohn & Sons of Stoke.

In 1957 the post office was rebuilt on site with the original frontage being retained.

The town's post office operation was transferred to the old MEB premises in Merrial Street in 1996.

29. Former John O'Gaunt's Castle Inn, Stanier Street, 1935

The original pub is not listed in a trade directory of 1822–23 but is listed in Cottrill's Police Directory of 1836 as the John O'Gaunt. It appears to have been rebuilt in 1872 and certainly had a bicycle club attached by 1880.

The pub was totally rebuilt by owners John Joule's & Sons Ltd, brewers of Stone, and reopened in August 1935. Its reconstruction took place at a time when breweries were expanding and numerous pubs were being built or rebuilt. Joule's also rebuilt the Saracen's Head in Meir in 1934 and the King's Arms in Meir in 1935. However, another trigger for the reconstruction of the Newcastle pub was the need to accommodate increasing road traffic through new roads. A report of the pub's opening commented significantly that the pub's yard 'can afford considerable car parking accommodation if required'. Road widening at Pool Dam necessitated the demolition of the old pub and the erection of the new John O'Gaunt's Castle Inn. The objective was to make Pool Dam a more impressive gateway into the town.

The pub was designed by Joule's architect J. S. Redman and built by the firm of Horace Poole of Newcastle.

The main frontage faced the corner of Pool Dam and Stanier Street. It incorporated red facing bricks and precast stone dressings and was roofed by Westmoorland slates. There were two entrances, one leading to the public bar and outdoor department and the other to the smoke room and lounge, above which there was a handsome oriel window.

In 1999, it became the Castle before being reopened in the spring of 2013 as the John O'Gaunt.

The front bar was a carpeted rectangle with the bar counter facing the main entrance. Bric-a-brac included a wooden model of a 'flying V' guitar while there

Above and below: Former John O'Gaunt pub, 2019.

was a distinct musical scheme elsewhere with references to The Who, the Stone Roses, the Rolling Stones and the Ramones.

By 2015 it was no longer operating as a pub but as the OneRecovery Centre for alcoholics. Nevertheless, the building still stands today as a reminder of the confidence of 1930s brewers and their architects.

30. Former Police Station, Merrial Street, 1936

This building replaced accommodation in High Street, part of the structure having comprised the original police office opened 102 years previously. These premises were seen as being outdated and inadequate for the requirements of the borough police in the wake of borough boundary extensions. Indeed, as Alderman A. Ryles noted in his book *A Positive Page* (1977), the new station in Merrial Street was built 'to accommodate the extra Wolstanton personnel added to the Newcastle Force, and the old police station came in for clearance'.

This said, the village of Wolstanton had its own police station near the top of Silverdale Road until around 1970, when policemen were transferred to Merrial Street. Leonard Brammer, born in 1940, who was employed by the special constabulary and afterwards the regular police at Wolstanton, told the

Below left: Former police station, 2019.

Below right: Former police station doorway, 2019.

author (interviewed in 2001) that 'After Wolstanton police station closed and we were transferred to Newcastle, it wasn't the same – they might as well have sent us to London.'

The old police premises in High Street, Newcastle, were duly demolished to create part of the space for the Lancaster Buildings.

The architecture of the new police station compared favourably with the beauty of the Municipal Hall, behind which it stood. Externally, it was 'designed with a civic character' and the chief architect was W. R. Davidge of London. Its style was neo-Georgian, and it incorporated a cupola.

Its main entrance was from Merrial Street, and there was a parade ground off the Municipal Hall yard. All rooms intended to receive the public were on the ground floor, with the inquiry counter being to the right upon entrance. Beyond the reception area was a general office and Chief Clerk's office. There was also a first-aid room, sergeant's room and parade room. The top floor embraced a lecture room and library, a uniform room and a wireless room that anticipated technological advancements in that direction. In 1947, the county council became the police authority.

In 2012, the police inquiry office was closed and reopened at the Guildhall in High Street.

31. Lancaster Buildings, High Street, c. 1940

A 1937 photograph shows the junction of Ironmarket with High Street and the block of buildings that stood on this site before the arrival of the Lancaster Buildings. This ornate range, incorporating quoined angles, accommodated the office of the Gas Department as well as Hamrogue's tobacconists.

The belief that Newcastle required further shopping facilities prompted the erection of the Lancaster Buildings on what had for some time been dubbed 'the Island Site' in High Street by the Newcastle Town Council.

The intention was to establish an impressive building accommodating shops and offices, and in 1935 the *Staffordshire Advertiser* newspaper stated that the council's General Purposes Committee had recommended that Mr Harry S. Fairhurst, the nominee of the president of the Royal Institute of British Architects, be appointed assessor in connection with the architectural competition for a design for the building. There was consultation with the occupiers of property in the adjacent area upon the suggested verandah or cantilevered cover over Cheapside. Hickton and Madeley of Walsall were eventually chosen as the architects in 1937.

The local press reported on the opening of the new £55,000 building in April 1940. It was completely steel framed with 14-inch brick main walls and floors of hollow tile and reinforced concrete construction. It embraced a dozen new shops as well as office space.

Above: Lancaster Building, 2018.

Right: Lancaster Building detail, 2018.

The sides of the art deco building featured roundels depicting aspects of local industry – a potter working at his wheel, a glass maker and some bottle ovens – bracketed by star motifs. 'The absence of unsightly pipes both inside and outside the building should be noted', suggested one journalist. 'Most of these have been placed in specially arranged ducts'.

In January 1943, Newcastle Borough Museum and Art Gallery opened in Lancaster Buildings. It was the first public building in Newcastle and exhibits included a copy of the Portland Vase by Josiah Wedgwood and specimens of seventeenth-century clay pipes.

A £2 million restoration and refurbishment of Lancaster Building was completed in 2010. It has been a Grade II listed building since 2005.

32. St Michael and All Angels Church, Linden Grove, Cross Heath, 1954

Standing on the outskirts of Newcastle, this Anglican church can trace its origins to 1877 when, during the time that Revd J. T. Jeffcock was the rector of St. Margaret's in Wolstanton (1867–77), a mission church was erected at Cross Heath.

Below and opposite: St Michael and All Angels Church, 2019.

In 1913, a local architect, F. R. Lawson, who had designed the still-extant model cottages on Moreton Parade, May Bank, unveiled by the Steel Smelters' Society in 1904, won a competition for the intended rebuilding of St Margaret's church.

However, this scheme was delayed by the First World War and never was pursued. Lawson's son, G. Forsyth Lawson, told the local press in 1954:

My father was a personal friend of Mr. Ellard, who was then lay-reader at Cross Heath, and together they carried out the first designs for Cross Heath church in 1937.

In 1938 my father was taken ill and the Parochial Church Council asked me to carry on. After the War, the Rev. D. Stevens and I got out a new design in view of the changed conditions of the parish, and just as we were able to begin the actual building, the designs had to be again completely changed owing to the probability of coalmining under the adjoining land.

It was this that dictated the whole shape of the church, and the Coal Board contributed a sum of money towards the cost of the foundations.

The church is built on a system of reinforced concrete beams like an egg-box, and there are two reinforced concrete girdles encircling the church above the nave arcade and above the main nave windows. Otherwise the church is constructed entirely of brickwork, using only lime mortar.

The roof trusses, he added, were of light steel construction in order to avoid lateral stresses on the supporting walls.

The bricks were supplied by Messrs Walley's of Silverdale, Rosemary Hill Tileries and Mr Caddick Adams gave all the quarry tiles laid in the church.

The architects were G. Forsyth Lawson and Cunningham and Partners of Banbury.

The present church continues to serve the community, holding coffee mornings and accommodating a Slimming World group.

33. Former Paulden's Department Store, High Street, 1957

The Manchester firm of Paulden's Ltd opened its first store in High Street, Newcastle, in 1946 – its first branch outside Manchester. It sold household goods including furniture and kitchenware.

However, in 1957 the rebuilt department store was launched on 10 May with a conspicuous splash advertisement in *The Sentinel* newspaper embracing a fine pen-and-ink illustration of the huge new store.

Throughout the conversion work, the store continued to trade, with various sections of the premises being sealed off to conceal building work. As their advertisement in the newspaper claimed at the time, 'Paulden's can rightly echo the famous claim of London's Windmill Theatre – "We Never Closed" '.

Former Paulden's site, 1994.

Former Paulden's site, 2019.

The main building contractors were Messrs. H. Brereton & Sons Ltd of Tunstall and Messrs C. H. Smith & Sons, Longton, assisted by Burton Constructional Engineering Company Ltd, of Burton-on-Trent, who designed fabricated and erected the steelwork. Hollington stone was incorporated in the façade. Numerous local firms were responsible for the internal decoration and fittings.

The shop published a departmental guide informing customers of the household goods and clothing to be found on the second floor, first floor, ground floor and basement.

The store, with its staff of 120, became massively successful and a leading retailer in Newcastle for many years as the town attempted to create an exciting and prosperous future. It rivalled the revered Henry White's stores and was built a few years ahead of the Castle House (United Co-op) department store in Ironmarket.

Inevitably it was a major employer and, reputedly, an enterprising one. In December 1960, the local press carried a reference to the Paulden's Choir giving Christmas concerts at both the Hillcrest Hostel in Wolstanton and the almshouses in Newcastle. Staff held Christmas parties at the nearby Castle Hotel, putting on concerts and doing comedy turns. They even held a Miss Debenhams contest for female employees.

In 1972, it was announced that Paulden's, which was by then a part of the Debenhams group, had begun trading under the Debenhams name. It continued to thrive.

In more recent years many retail premises have occupied parts of the building including Rymen's and Dixon's.

34. Former Woolworth Store, 1958

Frank Winfield Woolworth – having opened his first store in Liverpool in 1909 – opened his 300th store in Newcastle in 1928. It was housed in a half-timbered building that was formerly the Market Inn.

Upon examination of old photographs of the building and other half-timbered structures in Newcastle, we are reminded of the Tudor, and indeed mock-Tudor, buildings in Chester, many of which have been preserved to enhance the visual appeal of the town. However, as the 1960s approached, Newcastle's local authority showed very little interest in building conservation, and the efforts of the public and private sector produced a range of modern new buildings that were clinical and often brash. The reconstructed Woolworth's was one of the first High Street

F. W. Woolworth store, early 1970s.

Poundland, 2019.

stores to be modernised ahead of the radical changes in retail that occurred in the following decade. Work on it was completed in March 1958, though it never actually closed during the two and a half years of building work. During the excavations of the site, Stuart period coins and clay pipes were discovered.

When the store reopened, it was almost four times as large as its previous incarnation and was designed to provide a bright façade on the corner of High Street and Friar Street. Measuring 200 feet long by 50 feet wide, it was built with recessed doors at the front. The fascia sign boasted red and gold lettering, and there was a second entrance at the bottom of Friar Street. The building was 45 feet high in High Street, rising to 60 feet high in Friars Street. Two goods lifts connected the four stories of the building.

Internally, there was Terazzo tiled flooring and twenty-seven departments selling a far wider range of goods than its previous incarnation including – for the first time – Staffordshire-made china and earthenware as well as Staffordshire hardware. The number of staff rose from seventy-eight to 130 as a result of the reorganisation. Among the diverse items sold upon opening were Milady confectonary, Airfix model construction kits, Savoy assorted biscuits and Kingsmere canned foods, as well as Goldseal moth rings and air purifier.

The store closed in January 2009.

35. The Hollies Council Estate, Hempstalls Lane, 1961

Many people walk or drive past the Hollies without realising what an innovative scheme it was when set afoot in the early 1960s. The 4-acre estate comprised eleven blocks of four-storied flats, ten bungalows, twenty-six garages and a self-contained laundry, located on a sloping site that offered a wide view of the area from Keele to Chesterton.

It was built for Newcastle Corporation, the main contractors being Madew and Wardle Ltd of Market Lane, Newcastle. It was designed by Bourneville Village Trust, who were responsible for the Westlands housing development in the mid-1930s.

Described in the press as 'ultra modern', the dwellings incorporated underfloor heating, double-glazed and French windows open to railing balconies. A single aerial dispensed with 'the unsightly cluster usually seen on such buildings'. The laundry contained washers, spin dryers and airing cupboards. Some of the flats offered a special low bath designed with the elderly in mind.

By late 1961 the first residents moved into their new accommodation. The estate was built on a compact site, and it is interesting that John Briggs was to point out in his *Newcastle-under-Lyme 1173–1973* (1973) that 'it is unlikely that Council Houses will again be built on large estates'.

Below and opposite: The Hollies housing estate, 2019.

36. Former Shakespeare, George Street, 1963

The original Shakespeare stood in Brunswick Street and in the early nineteenth century incorporated a purpose-built cockpit that attracted sportsmen from Staffordshire, Cheshire and Derbyshire. The pub later moved to George Street, but the present building dates from 1963 and itself reflected changing tastes in leisure. It was a product of its time in its architecture and its concept.

The Shakespeare was opened on 18 July 1963 about a fortnight before the Seabridge in Clayton, with the brewers, Messrs Bass, Ratcliffe and Gretton Ltd, stating at the time: 'The new house is conveniently close to a large dance hall and the designers felt the character of the rooms should be kept as modern as possible with a view to inviting the rather younger people from the nearby ballroom ...'

For this reason the pub was built without a traditional bar, as it strove to attract the bright young things who patronised the adjacent Crystal Ballroom, which had opened in 1958 and had an underground ballroom, the Gold Mine, added in 1959. The role of this dance venue in encouraging the growth of pubs in the immediate area is seen in the fact that Ind Coope & Co. (West Midlands) opened

Above: Shakespeare pub, *c.* 1990. (Courtesy of Norman Scholes)

Below: Former Shakespeare, 2019.

the Bandstand (now the Rigger) in Marsh Parade in the autumn, and this might perhaps be viewed as a response to the arrival of Bass's Shakespeare.

There was first-floor manager's accommodation at the Shakespeare and there were two public rooms – the Avon Room and the Stratford Room. Built by Horace Poole Ltd, the floors boasted thermo-plastic tiles and some carpeting. The first licensees were Mr and Mrs Eric Alan Sumner, who sold draught Bass and Worthington E.

The Shakespeare was reopened under the cheap and nasty name of Billy's Boozer in 1997 and in 2001 became AJ's Sports and Entertainments Bar. The name changes may well have been an effort to mirror the various reinventions of the dance venue further up the street, whose later names included Tiffany's and latterly Zanzibar before its ultimate closure as an entertainment venue in 2004.

The building is now the Jalsa Indian restaurant.

37. Former Market Arcade, High Street, 1963

This structure, now incorporating the Vue Cinema, arrived in Newcastle as an expression of 1960s progressive thinking in the town.

Among the buildings that were demolished to make way for it were the Red Lion public house and the characterful mock-Tudor indoor market building of 1854, built of red brick with blue-brick decoration and embracing an oriel window and a crenellated parapet.

Village Shopping Centre, 1994.

Vue Cinema, 2019.

Work on the large new shopping development in Newcastle began in February 1962. It was a project set afoot by Arcade (Newcastle) Ltd and the Corporation. It opened in November 1963.

It was conceived as part of the zeitgeist of 'shopping under one roof' – a diametrically opposite shopping experience from browsing on The Stones, and another indicator of change in Newcastle.

There were two entrances from High Street, containing twenty-one shops. There were nine more shops in the basement.

The traffic factor of the 1960s was considered in this new development. It was built with drive-in facilities for vehicles serving the traders on the premises so that delivery vans did not have to park on the road outside. This was seen as an important safety aspect.

The façade was ultra-modern, too, yet it was claimed by the council at the time that the new development blended in with its neighbours – the Town Clerk's office on the left and the new Woolworth's on the right. The front of the building has now been altered from the time when it had a large grid of interconnecting geometrical shapes attached to it. This was described in an early advertising feature for the Arcade: 'The development faces the open street market and has an imposing façade with a large pierced reinforced concrete grille to the first and second floors.' To most men in the street, however, the building smacked of clinical functionalism.

Not all new shops were quite ready to trade at the time of opening, but the Market Arcade quickly became popular with Newcastle shoppers. Among the traders were the Capital Chinese and English restaurant, the radio and TV engineers A. J. Cadman, Tiko Pattiseries and Bill Davies's Mayfair gents' hairdressing salon.

38. Grosvenor Roundabout, High Street, 1965

This unusual piece of architecture reflects the major changes in communications that altered Newcastle's outlook and aspirations in the 1960s – and with it the built environment.

The A34 duel carriageway between Lower Street and Upper Green was constructed in 1965. In finding a solution to the contemporary problem of traffic congestion in the High Street, Newcastle had reached back to the past. The new road followed the approximate line of a pre-1826 road that ran from south to north via Stubbs Gate, Goose Street, Lower Street and Lower and Upper Green.

Grosvenor roundabout, 2017.

Grosvenor roundabout, 2019.

The Grosvenor roundabout originally incorporated a fountain, later replaced by a flower bed. The new two-lane duel carriageway cost £700,000 and was opened by Tom Fraser, the Minister of Transport, on 30 July 1965. The *Guardian* newspaper reported: 'This new highway, in spite of the presence of three roundabouts in its short length, should help to give the borough one of the most agreeably quiet centres in the country. Two years ago, the M6 removed a very large amount of through traffic going north-south along the A34; now the bypass – part of a five-mile improvement scheme – takes the remaining through traffic away from the Guildhall, the street market, and the main shopping centre.' Most of the north–south traffic was diverted to the western bypass in 1966, and by 1968 the High Street had been closed to all through traffic.

Over the years gardens in the sunken roundabout have proved to be a valuable resting place for harassed shoppers looking for a place to drop their shopping bags and sit for a while. As an open space in the town, it has been redeveloped at various times – and especially since the opening of the Safeway supermarket in the 1990s – through the addition of new grassed areas, brick-effect paving, concrete troughs, cast-iron railings and arches, hanging baskets and even a floral teddy bear, which was sadly ruined by vandals. Thus has a prime example of 1960s functionalism been allowed to develop as a much-loved town amenity.

39. St James' Church, Clayton, 1966

A pivotal figure in the arrival of the Anglican Church of St James the Great in Clayton was Revd Reginald Tozer, who as the press reported at the time 'had to adapt to the role of architect, decorator, designer, writer and secretary'. He wrote 3,200 appeal letters in 1964 and raised much money towards the church building fund.

The modest congregation had from 1950 met in a converted cow shed, though this arrangement kept many potential worshippers away, as, to quote Tozer, 'water seeped in through the floor and came down from the ceiling, and there was a distinct "cow-shed" odour'.

As part of the drive to finance the project, 'bricks' were sold to supporters for one shilling each – some of them to patrons of the Crystal Ballroom in Newcastle as they queued to get in.

It was Tozer's intention to build a modern Swedish-style building, which was ultimately consecrated on 29 April 1966. It has often been dubbed 'the church with the steep green roof'.

Newcastle Youth Club was based at St James' Church and the accompanying photograph shows a production of Aladdin, dated 1966/67. On the extreme left is George Harvey, who loaned the photograph, while Dougie Evans (second from the left) and Johnny Oakes (centre, with the hat) also appear.

St James' Church, Clayton, 2019.

St James' Church Youth Club members, 1966.

40. Midway Shops, Midway, 1966

Major road traffic developments in the centre of Newcastle in the 1960s triggered the demolition of some retail premises but was also to give rise to the creation of others. A new multistorey car park was erected in Lower Street in 1966. It survives today. It was built to ease car parking issues in the town centre but very soon afterwards a modest range of shops and offices were constructed on Midway in order to take advantage of the vehicle-borne custom that now arrived in that part of town.

The names of the new shops recall a bygone age in Newcastle. Rediffusion (West Midlands) offered their television showroom. Peter – 'Coiffures' – specialised in hair styling and hair pieces. Here also was Bryan's School of Motoring. The Music Salon was run by Roy Sylvester and his wife Kathleen, who were both musicians. This was the only shop in Newcastle to sell sheet music at the time and by 1970 it was also advertising 'records from 9/6 to 47/6, recorders, melodicas, auto harps and pianos'. The shop was advertised as being 'near the multi-storey car park', underlining how the town's new road system had been instrumental in partly redistributing retail footfall.

Above and below: Midway shops, 2019.

41. The Holiday Inn (previously the Post House Hotel), 1967

This hotel has been known as the Holiday Inn since 2001. It is not included in this book for its architectural merits but for what it represented in a rapidly changing Newcastle in the 1960s.

In a previous section, we have already recognised the importance of the Castle Hotel as one of the foremost community hubs of the town, but by the mid-1960s the hotel's days were numbered. Trust Houses, who owned the Castle as well as the Grand Hotel in Hanley, began building the Staffordshire Post House Motor Hotel in May 1966 on the Clayton Road junction with the M6 at Hanchurch. The group's projects manager, D. J. Mitchell, announced to the press that 'There was no intention to close the Castle Hotel.'

The new hotel – built on green belt – opened in September 1967, with fifty-three bedrooms and parking space for 118 cars. From the start it was geared towards motorway users requiring a stop-over venue – effectively the twentieth-century equivalent of the role of the Castle Hotel in the 1820s. Despite the earlier reassurances, the Castle Hotel closed in 1968, effectively replaced by a twentieth-century equivalent of the Castle as it served the town in the 1820s.

Below and opposite: Holiday Inn, Clayton, 2019.

42. York Place Shopping Centre, Red Lion Square, *c.* 1967

Red Lion Square changed drastically in the 1960s, not least because three architecturally attractive public houses were demolished.

The Hind's Vaults stood on the corner of High Street and Lad Lane. It was a timber-framed building with a double-gabled frontage. It was later faced with brickwork and given two projecting bay windows surmounted by cast-iron balustrades. Undoubtedly, it was one of the prettiest pub buildings in the town.

The Globe Commercial Hotel was a florid, brick and terracotta building with a heavily ornamented and shaped central gable. It had replaced a hostelry of the same name in 1898.

On the corner of Merrial Street stood the Central Hotel. These and neighbouring buildings were replaced by the York Place pedestrian shopping centre around 1967, which had a massive impact on the townscape.

The shops we see here today were built as part of the Laing Development Company's redevelopment scheme. They were erected on the corner of High Street and Merrial Street and among the early traders were Bookland, Craddocks, Cartwright & Co. (jewellers) and Martin's the Cleaners. This was ambitious new architecture for Newcastle, constructed from modern building materials. A Goliath of a building had appeared in the town.

Above: York Place, Lad Lane, 1994.

Below: Former Bookland and shops, 2019.

Forget the shaped front gables and the red brick and terracotta detail of the Globe Hotel. Newcastle's future had arrived – and Newcastle's future was concrete. The *Newcastle Times* newspaper described its architecture thus:

> The shop units will be contained within a reinforced concrete superstructure clad with dark brown facing brickwork and white precast concrete panels. Projecting from the face of the shop fronts will be a continuous concrete canopy with white pre-cast concrete upstands to coincide with the modular grid of the elevations.

Bookland opened in the new block of shops in 1967 and served the town wonderfully well, offering books, maps and stationery items such as fountain pens until its closure in 2005. As a high-quality bookshop, it is sadly missed.

A surviving (1973) photograph of York Place shows a large sign on the first floors advertising its thirty-one shops, 'all now reserved'.

43. Former Civic Offices, Merrial Street, 1967

Perhaps the most architecturally attractive building to be erected in the town centre in the 1960s, the Civic Offices were officially opened on 22 September 1967.

The building included offices, a council chamber, mayor's parlour, committee rooms and a council members' retiring room, allowing all the borough council's

Civic Offices, 1994.

Civic Offices, 2019.

departments to be housed under one roof for the first time. Previously they had been scattered around the town.

The *Newcastle Times* remarked that the staff and public had already become accustomed to the Merrial Street building.

With an Arnold Bennettesque mischievousness, the newspaper mused:

Those who live by the sword perish by the sword, and those who put on formal ceremonies are bound, in the same way, to suffer by formal ceremonies, for they are sure to offend someone. It didn't take long at Merrial Street on Friday to sense that something was wrong. Possibly it has something to do with the fact that half the councillors and their wives were in the Council Chamber itself and the other half were up in the public gallery. Perhaps the councillors out in the cold in the gallery thought all the wives should have been in the gallery and each councillor in his own earmarked seat down the chamber. After all, it's never pleasant to see someone sitting in your seat.

And adding to the feeling of disquiet experienced by the observer was the fact that at least three councillors were missing who would normally be expected to be seen there. And their absence was all the more marked when they didn't claim their seats for the luncheon afterwards at the Clayton Lodge ...

Why do the English have to have formal opening ceremonies? Merrial Street has been working smoothly for weeks now, and despite this little contretemps, will go on doing so in the years to come.

However, in 2018 history repeated itself and services from Newcastle Borough Council, Staffordshire County Council and the police, as well as Newcastle Library and registry office, all became housed under one roof at the new Castle House building.

The Civic Offices are intended to be demolished for the wider development of Ryecroft.

44. Former Newcastle Library, 1975

The date given here relates to the time when this building finally came to be used by the public.

It replaced the much-loved and beautiful Municipal Hall of 1890. Its demolition in 1966–67 was a running sore among many Newcastilians, probably guaranteeing that the building that replaced it would not be embraced by the public. The hall's clock mechanism was later housed in the library as a nod to the remote past, but is now to be found in Newcastle Museum.

The structure was completed long before 1975, after plans for its use as a department store fell through. Ultimately, Newcastle Central Library – formerly based in School Street – officially opened in the building on 12 June 1975. Figures released at the time indicated growing public approval of the service. 59,803 books were borrowed between 5 May and 7 June, a 32 per cent increase on the same period in 1974. Furthermore, the number of (vinyl) records issued had risen by 39 per cent.

Structural cracks in the library were first noticed during a routine survey in 1986 but further problems led to the second-floor administration block being evacuated and internal walls being removed in late 1990. Administration staff were temporarily transferred to the basement, though the library continued in use. However, in the early 1990s, the library temporarily relocated to the by-then vacant Castle House shop in Ironmarket so that structural repairs could be made to the building and concrete beams strengthened.

Afterwards, the library continued as a valuable education provider in Newcastle. However, whilst the standard of customer service was always excellent, standards visibly dropped, perhaps in the cause of being more customer friendly. Visitors consumed food and drink while accessing the computers in the reference room and often used what had once been designated the 'quiet study area' almost as a

Above and left: Former library, 2019.

social centre. Such are the ways in which library usage has changed over the years. There is presently no quiet study area in the library section of the new Castle House, where restricted space has necessitated a more open-plan arrangement, thus encouraging conversation among customers and staff moving from one part of the room to another.

45. New Victoria Theatre, Etruria Road, 1986

The Victoria Theatre originally opened in a disused cinema on the corner of Victoria Street, Hartshill, in 1962. It was the brainchild of Stephen Joseph and Peter Cheeseman.

Stephen Joseph had wanted a purpose-built theatre to be erected on the Brampton in Newcastle – particularly as he believed that patrons would not take theatre seriously in a converted building – but it was not until 1986 that the building, nestling in leafy surroundings, materialised.

The present 'New Vic' was Europe's first purpose-built theatre-in-the-round, with a seating capacity of 597.

The new building was designed to interface with its natural setting, as is clearly explained in an article written by the Staffordshire Wildlife Trust in 1990, telling

New Victoria Theatre, 2019.

New Victoria Theatre plaque, 2019.

of the project's beginnings and the signing of a lease on what had formerly been a Victorian garden overlooking Etruria Road. With 'the Vic's' reputation as a much-loved community theatre already secure, the then Theatre Director, Peter Cheeseman, liked the site and determined to build a theatre in a garden. Thus did wildlife conservation become an important element in the development of the location. Many mature trees were retained and the theatre was constructed to fit the site. The bricks were not chosen in the architect's office but in situ. Half a dozen small walls incorporating various bricks were built in order to see which would best blend in with the surroundings. A pond was dug out by volunteers and lined with butyl. It was planted with numerous water plants and soon attracted frogs. Soon there were twenty-two species of birds nesting around the site and a pair of blackbirds even built a nest on the bar balcony, rearing their young within a few feet of theatregoers.

More than 120 species of wild flower were planted including primroses, wild lily of the valley, woodruff and wood anemones.

Functionally, the building is first class, as it embraces a restaurant, coffee shop and conference/hire room. It also boasts of an education department and has staged numerous temporary art exhibitions, underlining the serviceability of the building as a cultural centre in North Staffordshire.

46. Former National Westminster Bank Regional HQ, the Brampton, 1988

When plans for this 19,000-square-feet scheme were submitted, it was claimed that it 'drove a coach and horses' through council policy of protecting conservation areas.

That said, the Brampton's architectural glories have long departed since many fine residences were built there in the nineteenth century, and today the tree-lined road accommodates a diverse range of buildings including Pitfield

Above and below: Former NatWest headquarters, 2019.

House, the Church of the Jesus Christ of Latter Day Saints and the Knight's legal services building.

In further mitigation, the neo-Georgian style of the building represents some attempt to harmonise with the elegance of this fine road.

In October 1991 it was announced that this £2 million building, employing seventy-eight people, was to close in order to cut costs as the recession began to hit.

The building has known a small number of vicissitudes since, as a plaque on its frontage indicates:

> Global banking and markets. RBS, the Royal Bank of Scotland. The UK operating centre opened on 14th September, 1992. Relaunched on 14th September, 2007 by David Shalders, Chief Operating Officer, RBS, Global Banking and Markets, and the Worshipful Mayor of Newcastle-under-Lyme, Councillor David Clarke.

The building presently stands empty in 2019.

47. Castle Walk Outdoor Shopping Area, off Ironmarket, 2001–04

Developer St Modwen created Castle Walk in several stages in conjunction with Newcastle Borough Council, which was, according to a feature in the *Sunday Sentinel* of 2002, keen to 'return to its roots by selling itself as a market town', thus illustrating once again the vacillatory approach of local government in Newcastle to the town's history, by turns embracing it and then wanting to sweep it under the carpet.

More recent reports in *The Sentinel* have cast doubts about the council's commitment to Newcastle as a market town, with stall holders on the Stones open-air market suggesting that officers need to be more supportive and to advertise the outdoor market more vigorously (*The Sentinel*, 16/2/2019]).

Castle Walk connects Ironmarket and Hassell Street and is intended, through its architecture, to blend in with other shops in the town centre. By December 2002, *The Sentinel* reported that the majority of the units in the £20 million development had been taken, with some retailers coming to Newcastle for the first time. Castle Walk was intended not to directly compete with neighbouring Hanley, but to emulate the success of similar market towns such as Congleton, Nantwich and Uttoxeter.

Castle Walk initially accommodated a number of impressive retail names such as Scott's, New Look, JJB Sports, Wilkinson's, Toni and Guy and Marks and Spencer's Simply Food branch.

Being in close proximity to the Stones, questions were asked concerning how the new development would impact on the outdoor market. Some traders suggested from the start that the bargain stores in Castle Walk were taking trade away from

Above and below: Castle Walk shops, 2019.

the marketers, while stallholder Paul Bailey told *The Sentinel* in 2019 that 'Castle Walk gets the footfall and people don't tend to come to this bit'.

Economic arguments aside, what Castle Walk does, through its attractive design and architecture, is provide a markedly different retail experience to that of the Stones on the High Street. It is a more intimate shopping area, though this has itself created occasional problems, with the council having to take a prohibitive stance on pavement advertising – the clutter created by A boards – in 2004.

48. Newcastle Community Fire Station, Knutton Road, 2011

Newcastle's new fire station opened on 31 August 2011, a state-of-the-art £4.5 million building and the eighth to be constructed by the Staffordshire Fire and Rescue Service under a £50 million private finance initiative.

It was constructed so to accommodate seventy firefighters as well as two fire engines, a targeted response vehicle and a water rescue unit.

However, with community use now being encouraged by the fire service, the venue soon became used by various groups requiring meeting accommodation, including the North Staffordshire Historians' Guild.

It was designed to be 'future proof" for sixty years. On 15 February 2012, a time capsule was buried beneath the station car park, containing a copy of *The*

Newcastle fire station (old), 2010.

Newcastle fire station (new), 2019.

Sentinel newspaper, photographs of firefighters and a copy of the birth certificate of Marcus Hancock, who was the first child to be born at Stoke University Hospital on 31 August, the day of the station's opening. The capsule, buried by Newcastle Mayor Trevor Hambleton, is scheduled to be opened fifty years after its burial.

The design of the building incorporates sharp angles and a roof overhang and is given a softer appearance with the conspicuous use of glass above and around the entrance.

49. The Cotton Mill Pub, Liverpool Road, 2014

According to its website, this pub's name recognises the town's former history of hat-making as well as silk and cotton mills. It is unusual for new-build pubs (other than those owned by Wetherspoon) to acknowledge the heritage of an area.

Felt hat-making was an important industry in Newcastle for over 300 years. There is a mention of a hatter in 1569, while in the 1830s over 520 men plied their trade in the hat industry.

A famous silk mill in Marsh Parade, Newcastle, was owned by William Henshall, 'silk throwster, dealer and chapman'.

Above: Cotton Mill pub/restaurant, 2019.

Left: Cotton Mill grounds, 2019.

The Directory of the Staffordshire Potteries (1818) informs us that a cotton manufactory was established between Chesterton and Newcastle in 1797. The story of Enderley Mills is told in *Secret Newcastle-under-Lyme* (2017, Mervyn Edwards), where mention is made of Richard Stanway, who opened his factory in Liverpool Road, Newcastle, in 1881, having already flourished as an outfitter, tailor and draper in High Street. He received contracts from central government including one that required him to manufacture uniforms for the British army. He became a leading employer in the town.

This Marston's pub opened on 24 November 2014 under the management of James Payton.

50. Castle House, Barracks Road, 2018

Castle House, Newcastle Borough Council's new headquarters, opened in July 2018 with the boast that it offered all council services under one roof.

Like so many local development sites, this one has an interesting back story, as it was formerly occupied by the St Giles' and St George's School building of 1895. Though derelict, it was felt worthy of preserving by many commentators, as it formed a perfect backdrop to the Queen's Gardens, also of the late Victorian period.

However, notwithstanding objections from heritage campaigners, the school was demolished in 2016 and the council erected the new building. Councillor Terry Turner told *The Sentinel*, 'If you want to stay in the Victorian age that is fine and dandy but I do not. Businesses are growing in the town, this is the next step.' Newcastle, however, continues to promote its historic buildings – at least those that have not been permitted to be demolished.

Councillors reasoned that the new hub building would make council services more accessible and would save taxpayers money in the long run by allowing older buildings to be vacated. Newcastle Library, registry office and the police are now based in the new building, albeit with less floor space than before. The once-magnificent reference library, a splendid resource for local and family historians, has been reduced to a pale shadow of its former self with only very limited space to store archive material. Much of this, therefore, was transferred to Stafford Record Office, making it far less available to elderly townsfolk or those without a private vehicle. Several of the retained reference books in the local history section of the library have been stolen, no longer being locked away in glass cabinets as they were in the old building.

The height of the building seems inappropriate to its location in what had been a beautiful Conservation Area and a credit to the town. Queen's Gardens – an open space that has been Newcastle's pride and joy since being laid out in 1899 – is now somewhat overshadowed by the council's new centrepiece, which occupies a gateway site in the town.

Above and left: Castle House, the Newcastle Borough Council hub, 2019.